T0209647

Titles by *Langaa* RPCIG

Francis B. Nyamnjoh
Stories from Abakwa
Mind Searching
The Disillusioned African
The Convert
Souls Forgotten
Married But Available

Dibussi Tande
No Turning Back. Poems of Freedom 1990-1993

Kangsen Feka Wakai
Fragmented Melodies

Ntemfac Ofege
Namondo. Child of the Water Spirits
Hot Water for the Famous Seven

Emmanuel Fru Doh
Not Yet Damascus
The Fire Within
Africa's Political Wastelands: The Bastardization of
Cameroon
Oriki'badan
Wading the Tide

Thomas Jing
Tale of an African Woman

Peter Wuteh Vakunta
Grassfields Stories from Cameroon
Green Rape: Poetry for the Environment
Majunga Tok: Poems in Pidgin English
Cry, My Beloved Africa
No Love Lost
Straddling The Mungo: A Book of Poems in English &
French

Ba'bila Mutia
Coils of Mortal Flesh

Kehbuma Langmia
Titabet and the Takumbeng

Victor Elame Musinga
The Barn
The Tragedy of Mr. No Balance

Ngessimo Mathe Mutaka
Building Capacity: Using TEFL and African Languages as
Development-oriented Literacy Tools

Milton Krieger
Cameroon's Social Democratic Front: Its History and
Prospects as an Opposition Political Party, 1990-2011

Sammy Oke Akombi
The Raped Amulet
The Woman Who Ate Python
Beware the Drives: Book of Verse

Susan Nkwentie Nde
Precipice

**Francis B. Nyamnjoh &
Richard Fonteh Akum**
The Cameroon GCE Crisis: A Test of Anglophone
Solidarity

Joyce Ashuntantang & Dibussi Tande
Their Champagne Party Will End! Poems in Honor of
Bate Besong

Emmanuel Achu
Disturbing the Peace

Rosemary Ekosso
The House of Falling Women

Peterkins Manyong
God the Politician

George Ngwane
The Power in the Writer: Collected Essays on Culture,
Democracy & Development in Africa

John Percival
The 1961 Cameroon Plebiscite: Choice or Betrayal

Albert Azeyeh
Réussite scolaire, faillite sociale : généalogie mentale de
la crise de l'Afrique noire francophone

Aloysius Ajab Amin & Jean-Luc Dubois
Croissance et développement au Cameroun :
d'une croissance équilibrée à un développement équitable

Carlson Anyangwe
Imperialistic Politics in Cameroun:
Resistance & the Inception of the Restoration of the
Statehood of Southern Cameroons

Bill F. Ndi
K'Cracy, Trees in the Storm and Other Poems

**Kathryn Toure, Therese Mungah
Shalo Tchombe & Thierry Karsenti**
ICT and Changing Mindsets in Education

Charles Alobwed'Epie
The Day God Blinked

G.D. Nyamndi
Babi Yar Symphony
Whether losing, Whether winning
Tussles: Collected Plays

Samuel Ebelle Kingue
Si Dieu était tout un chacun de nous?

Ignasio Malizani Jimu
Urban Appropriation and Transformation : bicycle, taxi
and handcart operators in Mzuzu, Malawi

Justice Nyo' Wakai:
Under the Broken Scale of Justice: The Law and My
Times

John Eyong Mengot
A Pact of Ages

Ignasio Malizani Jimu
Urban Appropriation and Transformation: Bicycle Taxi
and Handcart Operators

Joyce B. Ashuntantang
Landscaping and Coloniality: The Dissemination of
Cameroon Anglophone Literature

Jude Fokwang
Mediating Legitimacy: Chieftaincy and Democratisation in
Two African Chiefdoms

Michael A. Yanou
Dispossession and Access to Land in South Africa: an
African Perspevctive

Tikum Mbah Azonga
Cup Man and Other Stories

John Nkemngong Nkengasong
Letters to Marions (And the Coming Generations)

Straddling the Mungo:

A Book of Poems in
English & French

By

Peter Wuteh Vakunta

Langaa Research & Publishing CIG
Mankon, Bamenda

Publisher:
Langaa RPCIG
(*Langaa* Research & Publishing Common Initiative Group)
P.O. Box 902 Mankon
Bamenda
North West Province
Cameroon
Langaagrp@gmail.com
www.langaapublisher.com

Distributed outside N. America by African Books Collective
orders@africanbookscollective.com
www.africanbookscollective.com

Distributed in N. America by Michigan State University
Press
msupress@msu.edu
www.msupress.msu.edu

ISBN: 9956-558-89-3

© Peter Wuteh Vakunta 2009
First published 2009

DISCLAIMER

This is a work of fiction. Names, characters, places, and incidents are either the author's invention or they are used fictitiously. Any resemblance to actual places and persons, living or dead, events, or locales is coincidental.

Dedication

For global ethnic and linguistic minorities—aboriginal Australians, San people, American Indians, Pygmies, Maori and more.

Contents

"Chez nous, les rires comme les pleurs ont la force d'un fleuve en crue."
(Calixthe Beyala)

[In our culture, laughter and tears have the strength of a flooded river.]
(Calixthe Beyala)

Preface

In opting to write these poems in English and French, official languages of the Republic of Cameroon, I have elected to raise a strong voice against the wanton abuse of the constitutional provision that protects the country's official bilingual policy. Of the myriad critical issues that underlie what has been termed the 'Cameroon Anglophone Question', I believe that the language problem is by any measure the thorniest. Discourse on the issue of language in Cameroon is likely to open a can of worms. There is no language policy, to the best of my knowledge, put in place to forestall the marginalization of linguistic minorities. Consequently, the interpretation of the letter and spirit of the law is left to the whims and caprices of French-speaking judges who are ignorant of how the Anglo-Saxon judicial system functions. This has resulted in innumerable cases of miscarriage of justice. The language of training and daily routine in the military, police and gendarmerie is French, in stark contradiction of the national constitution which stipulates: "The State shall guarantee the promotion of bilingualism throughout the country. It shall endeavor to protect and promote national languages" (Article 1.3: 5). Anglophones can go to Hades if they do not understand French! That's the state of affairs in Cameroon. That is the 'Anglophone Problem' in plain terms. There is no turning a blind eye to this imbroglio because it will come back to haunt not just the present generation of Cameroonians but also those yet to be born.

The corollary of the linguistic question is the rift it has created between Anglophones and Francophones in Cameroon. Revolting disdain for the English language has led French-speaking Cameroonians to downplay the use of English as an official language although the constitution of the Republic is explicit: "The official languages of the Republic of Cameroon shall be English and French, both languages having the same status" (Article 1.3: 5). It should be noted that the second fiddle position assigned to the English language by French-speaking members of government has made the implementation of the nation's bilingual education policy a nonstarter. In English-speaking towns and cities in Cameroon such as Buea, Tiko, Kumba, Bamenda, Bali, Kumbo and Nkambe to name but a few, one finds billboards with inscriptions written in French only! At the Nsimalen International

Airport in Yaoundé one reads stomach-churning gibberish such as: "To gather dirtiness is good." One also finds on billboards inanities such as "Not to make dirty is better." This unintelligible trash is meant to be a word-for-word translation for "Ne pas salir c'est bien." The French in this sentence leaves much to be desired. But it is even more irksome to realize that there is no English language translation of the notices posted on the billboards. The authors of this unintelligible stuff know very well that in bilingual countries around the world, all official communication—billboards, memos, letterheads, road-signs, application forms, court forms, police documents, health forms, driver's licenses and hospital discharge forms—are all written in the official languages of the country in question. Failure to do so is tantamount to a transgression of the law, an illegal act punishable by law in any country where there is rule of law. I have no doubt at all that diplomats accredited to Yaoundé and other foreigners who visit Cameroon find our official language policy and its implementation utterly ludicrous.

Public authorities—mayors, governors, divisional officers, police officers and gendarmes—ought to maintain zero tolerance in upholding Cameroon's official bilingual policy, yet they are the greatest transgressors themselves. There is a pool of trained translators and interpreters at the Presidency of the Republic spending time on trivialities such as translating ballot-paper inscriptions for elections that are often rigged beforehand. Why not use them to perform this important task? These technocrats who were educated at the expense of the Cameroonian taxpayer should be made to serve the nation by translating official documents intended for public consumption. Administrative officials should avail themselves of the services of these well-trained professionals. Let myopia, bigotry and blind allegiance to an oligarchy at the helm not deter them from making use of the services of these communication experts.

It is my fervent hope that this bilingual anthology of poems would not only provide useful instructional material for educators but would also serve as an eye-opener to Cameroon's leadership and role-players. May it jerk them out of lethal inertia, and bring them to the realization that official bilingualism is not a pipe-dream but rather a powerful modus operandi with the potential to ease a myriad of socio-political bottlenecks.

Identity/Identité

Identity Crisis

I don't quite know who I am.
Some call me Frog
I still don't know who I am
My name is the Bamenda Man;
My name is Enemy in the House.
My name is the Biafran;
My name is underclass citizen;
My name is the black sheep of the family.
Shut up!
Don't bother me!
Don't you know that I am at home here?
You forget that I was born here.
I shall fight to my last breath,
To forge a real name for myself.
You shall call me Anglofrog!
You shall call me Franglo!

Shut up!
Don't bother me!
You forget that I am a son of the soil.
Don't you know I am in my birthplace?
I shall fight to the last drop of my blood
To forge a real lingo for myself!
I'll speak French;
You'll speak English
Together we'll speak Camfranglais;
Because we are at home in these precincts.
He who has ears should hear!

Crise d'identité

Je ne sais pas au juste qui je suis.
D'autres m'appellent Frog.
Je ne sais toujours pas qui je suis.
Mon nom c'est le Bamenda.
Mon nom c'est l'ennemi dans la maison.
Mon nom c'est le Biafrais.
Mon nom c'est le citoyen de second degré.
Mon nom c'est l'enfant terrible de la famille.
Taisez-vous!
Ne m'embêtez pas!
Vous ne savez pas que je suis ici chez moi?
Vous ignorez que je suis né ici.
Je me battrai jusqu'au dernier souffle
Afin de forger un nom véritable pour moi-même.
Vous m'appellerez Anglofrog!
Vous m'appellerez Franglo!

Taisez-vous!
Ne m'embêtez pas!
Vous ignorez que je suis du terroir?
Vous ne savez pas que je suis au berceau ?
Je me battrai jusqu'à la dernière goutte de mon sang
Pour forger une véritable langue pour moi-même!
Je parlerai Français,
Tu parleras Anglais,
C'est-à-dire qu'ensemble,
Nous parlerons le Camerounais
Parce qu'ici nous sommes tous chez nous,
A bon entendeur salut!

Indigenous Peoples

Who are we?
How many are we?
Where do we hail from?

We are the Ndobo——
Thirteen Autochthonous Peoples of Tikari Tribe.
Namely,
Meukoh——
Natives of the village of Bamunka.
Vengo——
Autochthons of the village of Babungo.
Nsei——
Indigenes of the village of Bamessing.
Papiakum——
Natives of the village of Baba I.
Shieh——
People of the village of Babessi.
Mbaw Yakum——
Natives of the village of Bambalang.
Ngwangleh——
Indigenous people of the village of Bangolan.
Perchop——
Natives of the village of Bamali.
Lunglue——
People of the village of Bafangi.
Mankong——
Autochthonous people of the village of
Bamunkumbit.
Kumbat——
Natives of the village of Balikumbat.
Gashu——
People of the village of Bali Gashu.
Gansing——
Autochthons of the village of *Bali* Gansing

See?
We are offfspring of one and the same mother!
Let'make peace!
Unity is strength.

5

Autochtones

Qui sommes-nous?
Combien sommes-nous?
D'où venons-nous?

Nous sommes les *Ndobo*—
Treize Peuples Autochtones de la Tribu Tikare.
A savoir,
Meukoh—
Originaires du village de Bamunka.
Vengo—
Autochtones du village de Babungo.
Nsei—
Indigènes du village de Bamessing.
Papiakum—
Natifs du village de Baba I.
Shieh—
Peuple du village de Babessi.
Mbaw Yakum—
Originaires du village de Bambalang.
Ngwangleh—
Indigènes du village de Bangolan.
Perchop—
Natifs du village de Bamali.
Lunglue—
Peuple du village de Bafangi.
Mankong—
Autochtones du village de Bamunkumbit.
Kumbat—
Indigènes du village de Balikumbat.
Gashu—
Originaires du village de Bali Gashu.
Gansing—
Peuple du village de *Bali* Gansing

Voyez?
Nous sommes les enfants de la même mère!
Faisons la paix,
Car l'union fait la force.

Fatherland

Whether you are Francophone
Or Anglophone
I don't care a fig!
We have one and the same fatherland.

Whether you are Bassa
Or Bami,
I couldn't care less.
We are born in the same country.

Whether you are Bafang
Or Beti,
It's all the same to me.
We belong in the same motherland.

You are Bakeweri,
And I am Bafanji
It boils down to the same thing.
We have the same fatherland.

You are Fulani,
And the other is Fang
Does that matter?
It does not change the fatherland!

You come from Wum
And she comes from Wouri,
It does not matter at all
You are all Ongolans!

Let's cease fire,
And make peace for the sake of our dear fatherland
Let's not split hairs!
United we'll stand.

7

Patrie

Que vous soyez Francophone
Ou Anglophone,
Je m'en moque comme de l'an quarante!
Nous avons une seule et même patrie.

Que vous soyez Bassa
Ou Bami[1],
Je m'en fous complètement!
Nous sommes nés dans le même pays.

Que vous soyez Bafang
Ou Beti,
Cela m'est égal.
Nous appartenons à la même patrie.

Vous êtes Bakweri.
Moi, je suis Bafanji,
Cela revient au même.
Nous avons la même patrie.

Vous êtes Foulbé,
Et, l'autre lui, est Fang,
Ça fait quoi?
Ça ne change pas la patrie.

Vous êtes originaires de Wum
Et elle est ressortissante de Wouri
Ca ne change absolument rien.
Vous êtes tous Ongolais[2].

Cessons de faire la guerre.
Faisons la paix au nom de notre chère patrie.
Il ne faut pas chercher la petite bête!
L'union fait la force.

---

[1] Abbreviation for Bamiléké.
[2] Adjective derived from the indigenous name of Cameroon, Ongola.

Afritude

A tiger does not proclaim its tigritude,
It jumps onto its prey.[3]
Me, I don't need to shout
In order to prove my Afritude
I am an African!
A tiger does not roar in order to prove its tigerishness.
Me, I don't have to ululate in order
To manifest my Afritude.
I am certainly an African!
Black and proud!

A tiger who proclaims its tigritude
Is a fake tiger.
I don't have to negotiate my Africanness.
I am completely African.

A lion roars
In order remind everyone
That he is king of the jungle.
I don't have to beat about the bush
In order to show that I am African.
Undoubtedly, I am African!
Son of the soil!

An elephant does not roar
To prove that he is the djintété of the kingdom.
I don't have to groan
To lend credence to my Afritude,
I am African!

A dog barks to vent its anger
I don't have to bark in a bid
To underscore my Africanness.
I am African!
Even the blind would testify.

---

[3] Statement attributed to Nigerian Nobel Prize Laureate, Wole Soyinka, reputed for having said: "A tiger does not proclaim its tigritude, its jumps on its preys." In his essay "Reparation, Truth and Reconciliation" (cf. *The Burde of Memory, the Muse of Forgiveness*, 1999).

Afritude

Un tigre ne proclâme pas sa tigritude,
Il saute sur sa proie.
Moi, je n'ai point besoin d'hurler
Afin de manifester mon Afritude.
Je suis Africain!
Un tigre ne rugit pas
Pour faire preuve de sa tigritude,
Moi, je n'ai pas besoin de crier
Pour de faire preuve de mon Afritude.
Je suis bien Africain!
Noir et fier!

Un tigre qui proclâme sa tigritude,
Est un faux tigre.
Moi, je n'ai pas besoin
De négocier mon Afritude.
Je suis tout à fait Africain!

Un lion mugit pour rappeler
À tout le monde qu'il est roi de la jungle.
Moi, je n'ai pas besoin de tourner autour du pot
Pour faire montre de mon Afritude.
Je suis sans doute Africain!
Fils du terroir!

Un éléphant barrit pour montrer
Qu'il est le djintété[4] du royaume;
Moi, je n'ai point besoin de gronder
Pour faire preuve de mon Afritude.
Je suis bien africain!

Un chien aboie pour
Manifester sa colère;
Moi, je n'ai pas besoin d'hurler
Afin de montrer mon Afritude
Je suis bien Africain!
Même les aveugles pourraient en témoigner.

---

[4] Boss, most powerful

Majunga Tok

I speak Majunga,
Because it pleases me.
Syntactic contructions make me feel dizzy!
I loathe grammar.

I express myself in Cam Tok,
Orthography is nightmarish to me!
I love street lingo.
I don't want to have anything to
Do with long-winded sentences,
Difficult to prononce!

I communicate in Camfranglais,
Verbal conjugation disgusts me!
I adore verbal infinitifs.

I haggle in Cameroonianism,
It is the language of the people.
Convoluted phraseology
Is a veritable Hades.

I speak Pidgin,
It is a language that suits us all.
It is not a slang reserved for the uneducated!

11

Majunga Tok

Je parle Majunga[5]
Parce que cela me plaît.
La construction syntaxique me donne le vertige!
Je déteste la grammaire.

Je m'exprime en Cam Tok.
L'orthographe m'est cauchemardesque!
Je tiens au langage terre à terre.

Je déteste les phrases longues
Difficiles à prononcer!

Je communique en Camfranglais.
La conjugaison verbale me fait horreur!
J'adore l'infinitif des verbes.

Je marchande en Camerounais[6].
C'est la langue du peuple.
Les phrases alambiquées
Sont mon véritable enfer.

Je parle Pidgin.
C'est une langue propre à nous tous.
Ce n'est pas un argot des analphabètes.

---

[5] Cameroon Pidgin English also called Cam Tok.
[6] Reference to Mercédès Fouda's book titled *Je parle camerounais: pour un renouveau francofaune* (Paris: Karthala, 2001).

Early Inhabitants

Every country,
Has its early inhabitants.
Australoids—
Are the autochthonous peoples of Australia.
Nomadic people comprising several tribes.

Every clime,
Has its natives.
San People also called 'Bushmen'—
Are the indigenous peoples of Southern Africa,
Inhabitants of the Kalahari Desert.

Every country,
Has its early inhabitants.
The Sioux also called 'American Indians'—
Are the autochthonous peoples of North America.
They are an ethnic minority restricted to the
Reservations.
They are a State within the State !

Every country,
Has its natives.
The Pygmies—
Are indigenous to Southern Africa, Central Africa,
And South-East Asia.
They are arboreal peoples!

Every clime,
Has its natives.
The Maori—
Are the indigenous peoples of New Zealand.

Premiers habitants

Chaque pays,
A ses peuples autochtones.
Les Australoids——
Sont les habitants autochtones de l'Australie.
Peuples nomades se composant de plusieurs tribus.

Chaque pays,
A ses peuples indigènes.
Les Sans dit 'Bushmen'——
Sont les natifs de l'Afrique australe,
Habitants du Désert Kalahari.

Chaque pays
A ses premiers habitants.
Les Sioux dit 'Indiens américains'——
Sont les peuples autochtones de l'Amérique du Nord,
C'est une minorité ethnique aux Etats-Unis
d'Amérique.
Cantonnés dans des Réserves.
C'est un Etat dans l'Etat!

Chaque pays,
A ses peuples indigènes.
Les pygmées——
Indigènes de l'Afrique australe, de l'Afrique centrale,
Du Sud-est Asiatique.
Domiciliés sur les arbres.

Chaque pays,
A ses peuples indigènes.
Les Maori——
Sont les natifs de la Nouvelle Zélande.

Franglo-Folly

You should know something about this,
Why do the French say:
Filer à l'anglaise?
We would like to know why.

You should know something about it,
Why do the English say:
To take a French leave?
We would like to know why.

You should know something about this,
Why do the Camfrogs say:
Les anglos sont gauches?
We would like to know why.

You should know something about this,
Why do the Camanglos say:
Frogs are myopic.
We would like to know why.

You should know something about this,
Why do the Camfrogs say:
Les anglos sont les biafrais.
We would like to know why.

You should know something about this,
Why do the Camanglos say:
Froggies are Francofools?
We would like to know why.
You should know something about this,
Why do Camfrogs talk of *Anglofolie?*
We would like to know why.

You must know something about this,
Why do Camanglos talk of Franco-folly?
We would like to know why.

My goodness!
How these people loathe one another!
Let's make peace!

Franglo-Folie

Vous devriez en savoir quelque chose.
Pourquoi les français disent:
Filer à l'anglaise?
Nous aimerions le savoir.

Vous devriez en savoir quelque chose.
Pourquoi les anglais disent:
To take a French leave?
Nous aimerions le savoir.

Vous devriez en savoir quelque chose.
Pourquoi les Camfrancos disent:
Les anglos sont gauches?
Nous aimerions le savoir.

Vous devriez en savoir quelque chose.
Pourquoi les Camanglos disent:
Les Camfrancos sont myopes?
Nous aimerions le savoir.

Vous devriez en savoir quelquechose.
Pourquoi les Camfrogs disent:
Les Camanglos sont les Biafrais
Nous aimerions le savoir.

Vous devriez en savoir quelque chose.
Pourquoi les Camanglos
Parlent-ils de la Francofolie?
Nous aimerions le savoir.

Vous devriez en savoir quelque chose.
Pourquoi les Camfrogs
Parlent-ils de l'Anglofolie?
Mon Dieu!
Que ces gens se détestent!
Faisons la paix!

Remonstrance/
Remontrance

Demo-Dictators

I am the State,
After me there will be a flood!
You know the proponents of this doctrine, don't you?
They are Africa's demo-dictators—
These dim-witted puppets
Who brand themselves 'enlightened leaders of the
people'!

I am the State,
These lame duck presidents
Who gained power thanks to electoral gerrymandering.
Certainly, you know them!

I am the State,
These neo-colonial accomplices,
So-called 'best pupils'[7] of the West.
Undoubtedly, you know them!

I am the State,
These pseudo-democrats of the Third World,
Who live at the expense of the 'wretched of the
earth'.
Obviously, you know them!

I am the State,
These dolls of maguida marabouts
Who live by the lie.
Kaï walahi! You sure know them!

---

[7] In a publication released by the National Secretariat of the Social Democratic Front (SDF), the writer underscores Paul Biya's lackey mentality in the following terms: "In the retrospective analysis of the end of Mr. Biya's reign, there will be many vignettes, like his declaration to a French journalist that he was the best pupil of Mitterrand..." (4)

Démo-dictateurs

L'Etat c'est Moi,[8]
Après moi le déluge!
Vous connaissez les tenants
De cette doctrine, n'est-ce pas?
Il s'agit des démo-dictateurs africains—
Ces marionnettes idiots
qui se nomment 'guides éclairés
du peuple'!

L'Etat c'est Moi,
Ces présidents officieux
Qui ont accédé au pouvoir
Grâce aux urnes bourrées.
Bien sûr, vous les connaissez!

L'Etat c'est Moi,
Ces complices des néo-colons,
Ces soi-disant élèves des
Présidents occidentaux.
Certes, vous les connaissez!

L'Etat c'est Moi,
Ces pseudo-démocrates du
Tiers Monde qui vivent aux dépens
Des 'damnés de la terre'[9].
Evidemment, vous les connaissez!

L'Etat c'est Moi,
Ces poupées des maguida[10] marabouts
Qui vivent dans le mensonge.
Kaï walahi![11] Vous devez les connaître!

---

[8] The credo of Louis XIV (1638-1715) of France. On this principle, he acted with intolerable inconsistency. He was popularly known as le Roi Soleil (Sun King) on account of his belief that just as the planets revolved around the sun, so too should France and the court revolve around him. His reign lasted seventy-two years, three months and eighteen days, the longest documented for any European monarch to date.

[9] Reference to Frantz Fanon's classic titled *Les damnés de la terre* (Paris: François Maspero, 1968)

[10] Person who hails from one of the Northern Provinces in Cameroon.

[11] Ideophonic expression conveying surprise in Fulfulde, a language spoken in Northern Cameroon.

The Downtrodden

They are left alone to face their sad fate,
The downtrodden of this world.
What is the fate reserved for the handicaped?
Those who have neither hands nor legs?
We leave them to their own devices !

They are left alone to face their sad fate,
The underprivileged of this world.
Those who own neither property nor money.
We leave them to struggle on their own!

They are left alone to face their terrible fate,
The famished of this world.
Those who cannot afford a meal to eat.
We allow them to manage on their own!

They are left alone to face their unbearable fate,
Those who have no roof over their heads,
Those who sleep in cardboards in the streets.
We allow them to sort things out for themselves.

They are left alone to face their unimaginable fate,
The orphans of this world.
Those who have neither father nor mother.
We let them find a way out on their own!

They are left alone to face their unfathomable fate,
The sickly of this world.
Those who are in bad health.
We allow them to suffer in pain.

They are left alone to face their horrendous fate,
The oppressed of this world.
Those who are victims of injustice.
We allow them to bear the brunt of miscarriage of justice!

Honestly,
This world is dreadful
Let's live in hiding!

Les damnés de la terre

Ils sont abandonnés
A leur triste sort.
Les damnés de cette terre.
Quel sort réserve-t-on
Aux handicapés du monde?
Ceux qui n'ont ni main ni pied?
On les laisse se débrouiller!

Ils sont abandonnés
A leur malheureux sort,
Les déshérités de ce monde:
Ceux qui n'ont ni propriété ni argent.
On les laisse se défendre!

Ils sont abandonnés
A leur horrible sort,
Les affamés de cette terre:
Ceux qui ne mangent guère à leur faim.
On les laisse se débrouiller!

Ils sont abandonnés
A leur insupportable sort,
Les sans-abris de ce monde:
Ceux qui dorment dans des cartons à la rue.
On les laisse se débrouiller!

Ils sont abandonnés
A leur incroyable sort,
Les orphelins de cette terre:
Ceux qui n'ont ni père ni mère.
On les laisse se débrouiller!

Ils sont abandonnés
A leur impensable sort,
Les maladifs de ce monde:
Ceux qui sont en mauvaise santé.
On les laisse souffrir en douleur!

Ils sont abandonnés
A leur terrible sort,
Les opprimés de cette terre:
Ceux qui sont victimes de l'injustice
On les laisse supporter le poids du manque de justice!

Vraiment,
La terre-ci est épouvantable,
Vivons en cachette!

Africa, Oh My Africa!

They are legion,
These puppet presidents
Grave-diggers of the nation!
I am the State.
Yes, they are many.

They are numerous,
These demo-dictatorial heads of government
People's grave-diggers
We are the State.
Undoubtedly, there are many of them.

They are so many,
These pseudo-intellectual leaders
Enemies of the State.
We are the State.

There are tons of them,
Rogue governors
Who pilfer from State coffers.
They are anti-people.

There are lots of them
Those leaders bereft of common sense.
They are fraudsters
Who make believe they are governing.

Oh, Africa,
My beautiful people!
Live and let live!

Afrique, Ah Mon Afrique!

Il y en a beaucoup,
ces chefs d'Etat marionnettes.
C'est des fossoyeurs de l'Etat.
L'Etat c'est moi.
Oui, ils sont nombreux.

Il y en a nombreux,
ces chefs de gouvernement
démo-dictateurs.
C'est des fossoyeurs du peuple.
L'Etat c'est nous.
Evidemment, il y en a beaucoup.

Il y en a tant,
ces dirigeants pseudo-intellectuels.
C'est des ennemis de l'Etat.
L'Etat c'est nous.

Il y en a tellement,
ces gouverneurs pillards
de l'Etat.
C'est des anté-peuples

Il y en a beaucoup
ces leaders dépourvus
de bon sens.
C'est des faussaires
Qui font semblant de gouverner.

Ah, Afrique,
Mon beau peuple!
Vivons seulement!

News Briefs

It feels like Planet Earth
is a mental asylum
Daily occurrences bear testimony.

Not a single day goes by
Without some news about
Multiple bizarre incidents.

Our men in the cassock
Are no longer servants of God.
No, they are pedophiles!

Our politicians
Are no longer the spokesmen of the people
No, they are looters
Of the national bread basket!

Our teachers
Are no longer dispensers of knowledge,
No, they are degree merchants!

Our students
Are no longer in quest of knowledge
No, they are drug and sex traffickers!

Our doctors
Are no longer life-savers.
No, they are abortionists!

Someone once said that
This world of ours is macabre,
Let's be on our guard!

Faits divers

On dirait que la Planète Terre
est un asile d'aliénés.
Des faits divers quotidiens
en font témoignage.

Aucun jour ne se passe
sans que l'on entende parler
de multiples faits insolites.

Nos hommes en soutane
ne sont plus les serviteurs de Dieu.
Mais non, c'est des pédophiles!

Nos hommes politiques
ne sont plus les porte-paroles du peuple.
Mais non, c'est des pilleurs
de la mangeoire publique!

Nos enseignants ne sont plus
les fournisseurs de la connaissance.
Mais non, c'est des marchands de diplômes!

Nos élèves
ne sont plus des chercheurs de la connaissance.
Mais non, c'est des trafiquants
de drogues et de sexe!

Nos médecins ne sont plus
les garants de la vie.
Mais non, c'est des avorteurs!

Le monde-ci bas est macabre,
Comme dit l'autre.
Vivons sur le qui-vive!

Civilizing Mission

We're white and powerful;
You're neither white nor powerful.
Do you realize that?

We're very civilized;
You're savage illiterate people.
Are you aware of this?

Your world is a tabula rasa,
With neither knowledge nor mores.
Did you know this?

We're God's special envoys
Charged with the sacred mission
Of civilizing your benighted world.
Did you know this?

Do not go away with the impression
That we're schemers or something like that.
No, no! Ours is a benevolent mission.

We have nothing to do with your oilfields,
We don't give a damn to your gold mines,
We couldn't care less about your mineral resources,
Because that has nothing to do with our civilizing
mission!
The goal is quite immaterial.
I hope you get it!

Mission civilisatrice

Nous sommes blancs et puissants;
Vous êtes ni blancs ni forts.
Vous vous en rendez compte?

Nous sommes bien civilisés;
Vous êtes sauvages et analphabètes.
Vous vous en rendez compte?

Votre monde est une table rase,
Sans connaissance ni moeurs.
Le savez-vous?

Nous sommes des envoyés spéciaux de Dieu,
Chargés de la mission sacrée de
Civiliser votre monde ténébreux.
Vous vous en rendez compte?

N'allez pas vous imaginer que nous sommes des
Magouilleurs ou quelque chose de ce genre.
Non et non! Notre mission est tout à fait bénévole.

On se fiche de vos gisements pétrolifères!
On s'en fout de vos mines d'or!
On se moque de vos ressources minérales!
Parce que ça n'a rien à voir avec notre mission
civilisatrice!
La mission est bien désintéressée.
J'espère que vous pigez!

Topsy-Turvy World

I would like to know
Why children nowadays
Love early sexual relations.
I believe it's because they'd love
To turn things upside down!

I would like to know
Why adolescents of today
Smoke marijuana and do drugs in public.
It seems to me that's because they are shameless.
They'd love to see the world topsy-turvy!

I would like to know why
Nowadays kids have taken to pornography
It appears it is because they lack morals.
They'd love to see the world in a shambles!

I would like to know why
Minors consume alcohol without qualms
It seems to me that they're badly brought up.
They would love to see the world upside down!

I would to know why
The youths of today dress so badly.
I believe their demeanor is an insult to propriety.
They would love to put things out of order!

I would like to know why
Youngsters have a predilection for firearms.
I think it is because they love jungle justice!
They would like to make the world uninhabitable.

And what about us, adults?
Are we positive role-models?
We'd do better to ask each other this question!

Monde à l'envers

J'aimerais savoir la raison
Pour laquelle les jeunes de nos jours
adorent la copulation précoce.
Il me semble que c'est
Parce qu'ils tiennent à tout mettre sens dessus dessous.

J'aimerais savoir pourquoi
les adolescents de nos jours
fument le chanvre indien
et consomment la drogue en public,
Il me semble que c'est
parce qu'ils n'ont pas honte.
Ils aimeraient à tout mettre en cafouillage.

J'aimerais savoir la raison
pour laquelle les gosses de nos jours
aiment la pornographie.
Il me semble que c'est
parce qu'ils manquent de moralité.
Ils aimeraient tout mettre en désordre.

J'aimerais savoir pourquoi
les enfants de bas âge
boivent de l'alcool sans gêne.
Il me semble que c'est
parce qu'ils sont mal élevés.
Ils tiennent à tout mettre à l'envers.

J'aimerais savoir la raison
pour laquelle les gamins de nos jours
s'habillent si mal.
Il me semble que c'est un outrage à la pudeur.
Ils aimeraient tout mettre sens dessus dessous.

J'aimerais savoir
pourquoi les jeunes de nos jours
ont la prédilection pour les armes à feu.
Il me semble qu'ils adorent

faire la loi dans de la jungle.
Ils aimeraient rendre le monde invivable..

Et nous autres, les adultes?
Sommes-nous de bons exemples?
Il faudrait se poser la question, les uns aux autres!

Slavery

Are you conversant with this word?
What does it mean?
Who is a slave?
It's a person in chains, isn't that right?
Not necessarily!

One could be free and enslaved
At the same time:
A dipsomaniac is a slave to alcohol.
Did you know that?
A smoker is a slave to tobacco
Did you know that?
A drug addict is a slave to drugs.
Did you know that?
A glutton is a slave to food.
Did you know that?
A miser is a slave to his money.
Did you know that?

A narrow-minded person is a slave to his own ideas.
I am sure you knew that.
An atheist is a slave to Satan.
I am sure you knew that as well.
A nymphomaniac is a slave to his sexual desires.
Undoubtedly, you knew that.
A racist is a slave to his prejudice.

Here then, is a word fraught with meaning.
It is prudent to always think twice
before using a word.

31

Esclavage

Connaissez-vous ce mot?
Qu'est-ce que c'est?
Qu'est-ce que c'est qu'un esclave?
C'est une personne enchaînée, n'est-ce pas?
Pas forcément!

On pourrait être à la fois
Libre et esclave:
Un dipsomane est esclave de l'alcool.
Le saviez-vous?
Un fumeur est esclave du tabac.
Le saviez-vous?
Un drogué est esclave de la drogue.
Le saviez-vous ?
Un gourmand est esclave de la bouffe.
Le saviez-vous?
Un avare est esclave de ses sous.
Le saviez-vous?
Un borné est esclave de ses propres idées.
Vous le saviez certainement.
Un athée est esclave de Satan;
ça vous le saviez également!

Un nymphomane est esclave
de ses désirs sexuels;
Sans doute, vous le saviez.
Un raciste est esclave de ses préjugés.

Voici donc, un mot bien ambigu.
Il faut toujours réfléchir
Avant d'utiliser un mot quelconque.

Mental Asylum

I am asking the same question
for the umpteenth time:
Are we in a mental asylum?
What is this jungle where
Kith and kin are at daggers drawn?
What is wrong with us?
We have all lost our minds!
We are all crackpots!

War! War! War! Everywhere!
What's the matter?
It feels like a mental asylum.
Filled with lunatics.
In the beginning God created human beings in His
image.
He created them to love one another.

Yes, He created human beings
In His own image!
He created man and woman.
God blessed them saying:
Be fertile, go yee and multiply,
Fill the earth,
And be masters.
Is there a misunderstanding?
God enjoined humans to dominate the fishes,
Seas, birds in the air
And all the reptiles and insects,
God never gave man the leeway to kill man!
Let reason prevail!

Asile d'aliénés

C'est la énième fois que je me pose
la même question.
Sommes-nous dans
un asile d'aliénés?
Quelle est cette jungle
où les frangins
sont à couteaux tirés?
Qu'est-ce qui nous arrive?
Nous avons tous
perdu la boussole!
Nous sommes cinglés!

Guerre! Guerre! Guerre! Partout!
Qu'est-ce qui ne va pas?
J'ai le sentiment
d'être dans un asile
d'aliénés plein à craquer des mabouls.
Au commencement,
Dieu créa les êtres humains pour qu'ils
soient à son image.
Il les créa pour qu'ils s'aiment, les uns les autres.

Oui, il les créa pour qu'ils
soient à sa propre image!
Il les créa homme et femme.
Dieu les bénit en disant:
Soyez féconds, multipliez-vous,
Remplissez la terre,
Rendez-vous en maîtres.

Y-a-t-il malentendu?
Dieu nous a ordonné de
dominer les poissons,
Les mers, les oiseaux du ciel
et tous les reptiles
et les insectes.
Dieu n'a point du tout ordonné
à l'homme d'abattre l'homme.
Soyons sages!

34

Drunkard

Woe tide you drunkard!
You who stay up late to drink matango.
Shame on you drunk!
You who go from bar to bar looking for jobajo to drink.
Stop gazing lovingly at majunga,
As it sparkles in your glass.
It will descend easily into the stomach
But will end up biting you like a snake.
It will stink you like a viper.
Shame on you drunk, alcohol lover!

Woe betide you, 33 Export drinkard!
You who go from circuit to circuit
In search of strong drinks to wet your throat.
Your eyes will see strange things.
You will have the feeling of lying in an open sea,
Tossed about like a sailor on top of a mainmast.

Issssshhh ! Matango!
Pwaaaaahh ! Odontol!
Uooouuuffff Jobajo!
Wuuussshh ! Majunga!
Enemies of the stomach!

Soûlard

Malheur à vous, soûlard!
Vous qui restez tard à boire du *matango*.[12]
Vous dévriez en avoir honte, ivrogne!
Vous qui parcourez les bars en quête du *jobajo*.[13]
Ne couvez pas de vos regards le *majunga*[14]
Quand il brille de son éclat dans votre verre.
Il descend si aisément dans le ventre,
Mais finit par vous mordre comme un serpent
Et vous piquer comme une vipère.
Vous dévriez en avoir honte, amoureux d'alcool!

Malheur à vous, buveur de la 33 Export!
Vous qui marchez de circuit[15] en circuit
En quête de vin et spiritueux pour vous mouiller la gorge.
Vos yeux verront des choses étranges
Et vous laisserez échapper des paroles incohérentes.
Vous avez l'impression d'être couché en pleine mer,
Ballotté comme un matelot en haut d'un mât.

Issssshhh ! Matango!
Pwaaaaahh ! Odontol!
Uooouuuffff Jobajo!
Wuuussshh ! Majunga!
Ennemis du ventre!

---

[12] Palm wine
[13] Beer
[14] Locally distilled whisky
[15] Beer parlor in a private residence

Cruel City

In our country
We live on the alert,
Gripped by fear of torturers—
Mange-milles devoid of shame
Who steal in broad day light.

In Ongola,
Everyone lives in hiding
Because of swindling gendarme officers
And illiterate zangalewa[16]
Who are unbearably brutal.

At home,
We live at the mercy of criminals,
Many of them university graduates,
Working in collusion with law enforcement officers
To terrorize and burgle civilians.
We are sick and tired of forces of law and order
Who turn a blind eye to crime.

At home,
We live in fear,
Caused by an outrageous dictatorship—
Puppet heads of State
Totally deprived of intelligence!

In Ongola,
We have had enough of torture,
We have had enough of dictatorship,
We have had enough of swindling,
We are sick and tired of window-dressing,
We are not the 'wretched of this earth'[17]!

---

[16] Soldiers
[17] Reference to Frantz Fanon's classic *The Wretched of the Earth* (New York, Grove Press, 1963)

Ville cruelle[18]

Chez nous,
On vit sur le qui-vive,
De peur des tortionnaires—
Des mange-milles[19] déhontés
Qui volent en plein jour!

A Ongola,
Tout le monde se cache,
A cause des gendarmes escrocs
Et des zangalewa analphabètes
On ne peut plus brutaux!

Au bercail,
On vit à la merci des malfaiteurs,
En majorité des diplômés d'universités,
Travaillant avec la complicité des forces de l'ordre,
Pour terroriser et dévaliser les populations.
Nous en avons marre des hommes en tenue
Qui ferment les yeux sur les actes criminels.

Au pays,
On vit dans la peur
Semée par la dictature outrancière—
Des chefs d'états polichinelles
On ne peut plus stupides!

A Ongola,
On en a marre de la torture!
On en a assez d'escroquerie!
On en a ras le bol de tromperie!
Nous ne sommes pas les damnés de cette terre!

---

[18] Calqued on Eza Boto's novel *Ville cruelle* (1954)
[19] Derogatory name for corrupt Cameroonian policemen.

38

Down With Kleptomaniacs!

Rigor and moralization
Go ahead, Mbiya!
Go ahead Father of the Nation
We are behind you.
Go ahead National Guide,
We support your action
With faith and unity.

Rigor and moralization
Eat your share Mbiya!
The trough is inexhaustible
Just eat your share
Grave-digger of the Nation!
Eat your share with rigor and immorality.
We support your inaction
Of infidelity and off-handedness.
Eat your part with rigor and infatuation
Eat your share and leave us in alone.

Assume the task Mbiya
Father of the ghost-nation
Eat your share Mbiya!
Always sexy guy.
Do not relent in your mission of dilapidation
With rigor and determination.
You are God's gift to us
Pursue your mission
We are behind you.
What can we do?
Down with thieves!
Down with kleptomania!
Long live rancor and immorality!

A bas les kleptomanes!

Rigueur et moralité
Va de l'avant, Mbiya!
Va de l'avant Père de la nation
Nous soutenons ton action,
Va de l'avant Guide national
Nous soutenons ton action
De foi et d'unité.

Rigueur et moralité
Mange ta part Mbiya!
La mangeoire est inépuisable.
Mange ta part seulement,
Fossoyeur de la Nation!
Mange ta part avec rigeur et immoralité.
Nous soutenons ton inaction
D'infidélité et de désinvolte.
Mange ta part avec rigeur et engouement
Et laisse nous tranquilles seulement.

Assume la tâche Mbiya
Père de la nation-fantôme,
Mange ta part Mbiya!
Toujours chaud gars.
Continue ta mission de la déconstruction
Avec rigueur et fermeté.
C'est Dieu qui te nous a confié.
Continue ta mission.
Nous sommes avec toi.
On va faire comment, alors?
A bas les voleurs!
A bas la kleptomanie!
Vive la rancune et l'immoralité!

Waiting For The Messiah

You must be patient
Where are you hurrying to?
We're waiting for the Messiah.
The Messiah is not coming
Let's keep waiting,
One day he will come.
The nation is waiting
The wife is waiting,
The husband is waiting,
The offspring are waiting
We're all waiting.
You must wait longer!
Ours is a nation of "Wait and see".
One of these days,
He will come to deliver us.

En attendant le Messie

Il faut patienter
Vous vous pressez pour aller où?
On attend le Messie!
Le Messie n'arrive pas!
Attendons seulement,
Un jour il viendra.
Le pays attend
La femme attend,
Le mari attend,
Les enfants attendent,
On attend tous.
Il faut persister dans l'attente!
On vit dans un pays en sursis.
Un de ces quatre matins,
Le Messie viendra nous délivrer.

High-Speed Train (HST)

S.O.S! Help!
We're aboard an HST,
High speed train,
Running at a breathtaking speed.
We need stop lights!

S.O.S! Help!
We're on an HST,
Where minors are making babies
Before our very own eyes.
We need stop lights.

S.O.S! Help!
Welcome aboard our HST,
Where teenagers are totting guns at random
We need stop lights to put an end to this madness!

S.O.S! Help!
Welcome to our HST,
Where baby-mothers are getting rid
Of their newborns by dumping them into dumpsters.
We need stop lights to stop this lunacy!

S.O.S! Help!
We are on an HST,
Where school kids trade
hard drugs with impunity
We need stop lights to end this insanity!

S.O.S! Help!
We are aboard an HST,
Where divorce has become common currency.
We need stop lights to bring this imbecility to an end!

S.O.S! Help!
We are on an HST,
Where God is on vacation.
We need stoplights to stop this skidding!

Train à grande vitesse (TGV)

Au secours! Au secours!
Nous sommes à bord d'un TGV,
Train à grande vitesse,
roulant à une vitesse vertigineuse.
Il nous faut des feux rouges!

Au secours! Au secours!
Nous sommes à bord d'un TGV
où les mineurs se fabriquent
des bébés à vue d'oeil.
Il nous faut des feux rouges!

Au secours! Au secours!
Bienvenus à bord de notre TGV
où des gamins tripotent des armes à feu au hasard.
Il nous faut des feux rouges
Pour mettre fin à cette folie!

Au secours! Au secours!
Soyez les bienvenus à bord de notre TGV
où des fille-mères se débarrassent
de leurs nouveaux-nés dans les latrines.
Il nous faut des feux rouges
pour arrêter cette déraison!

Au secours! Au secours!
Nous sommes à bord d'un TGV
où des écoliers commercialisent
de la drogue en toute impunité.
Il nous faut des feux rouges!
pour arrêter cette démence!

Au secours! Au secours!
Nous sommes à bord d'un TGV
où le divorce est monnaie courante.
Il nous faut des feux rouges!
pour mettre fin a cette imbécilité!

Au secours! Au secours!
Nous sommes à bord d'un TGV

où Dieu est en congé.
Il nous faut des feux rouges!
pour arrêter ce dérapage!

Witchcraft

My dear friend,
Do not bewitch me for the sake of love.
Love cannot be coerced!

My dear brother,
Do not sell me in *famla* to get rich
Wealth comes from God.

My dear cousin
Do not sell in moyongo.
Filial relationship is not a commodity!

My dear sister,
Do not practice sorcery on me
because of *chop-chair* palaver
Inheritance is the right of the eldest
It has nothing to do with hop-eye!

Ma dear tara,
Do not practice voodoo on me
For the sake of frienship.
You can't force friendship!

My sweetheart
Do not use tima-mboussa on me
because of marriage.
You can't force marriage!

My dear wolowoss,
Do not put mbongo chobi in my food.
Prostitution is not witchcraft!

My magician nephew,
Do not sell me into Koupe,
Kinship should not be commericialized!

Maraboutage

Ma chère amie,
Ne me fais pas la sorcellerie à cause de l'amour!
L'amour n'est pas forcé.

Mon cher frère,
Ne me vend au famla[20] à cause de la richesse.
La richesse provient de Dieu.

Mon cher cousin,
Ne me vend pas au muyongo[21]!
La parenté n'est pas une marchandise!

Ma chère soeur,
Ne me fais pas le maraboutage
à cause de l'affaire chop-chair[22]
L'héritage c'est le droit d'aîné!
Il ne s'agit pas de hop-eye[23]

Mon cher tara[24],
Ne me fais pas le vaudou!
L'amitié n'est pas forcée.

Ma chérie coco,
Ne me fais pas le tima-mboussa[25]!
Au cause du mariage.
Le mariage n'est pas forcé.

Ma chère wolowoss,
Ne me mets pas le mbongo-chobi dans la bouffe![26]
La prostitution n'est pas sorcière!

---

[20] Bamileke secret society noted for acts of sorcery
[21] Witchcraft
[22] Heir
[23] Bullying
[24] Friend
[25] Love potion in Cameroon.
[26] Love potion in Cameroon

Mon neveu magicien,
Ne me vend pas au Koupé[27]!
La parenté ne se marchande pas!

Empty Vessels

Trust your elected representatives,
Your roads will soon be tarred,
Within the means at their disposal.
A promise is a debt!

Have confidence in your MPs,
All the hospitals will soon have
Supplies of medication
within the limits of what is possible.
A promise is a debt!

Rest assured,
All the degree holders working in Chômecam
Will be employed as soon as possible,
within the limits of what is possible
This sort of misery should be taken seriously!.

This is for sure,
All salary arrears shall be paid immediately,
Within the limits of our means.
You cannot sleep when your
Neighors are starving.

Trust us,
All your schools shall soon be furnished
with learning resources
Within the limits of our budgets.
A promise is a debt!

---

[27] Cameroonian secret society

It's certain.
All retired workers shall be catered for
Without any other form of ceremony.
No one shall spend months vegetating in front of
the Nation Insurance Building.
A promise is a debt!

It goes without saying,
All the homeless shall be given homes
Without further ado.
We live in conformity with
the dictates of the Social Contract!
A promise is a debt!

You must always believe
That which your elected representatives tell you!
Even if they are laughing up their sleeves.
They are not empty vessels,
You shouldn't joke about them, hein!

Bidons vides

Faites confiance aux élus du peuple,
Vos routes seront goudronnées d'ici peu,
Dans les limites de leurs moyens.
Chose promise, chose due!

Fiez-vous à vos députés,
Tous les hôpitaux seront
Approvisionnés en médicaments,
Dans les limites du possible.
La promesse est une dette!

Rassurez-vous,
Tous les diplômés travaillant au Chômecam[28]
Seront embauchés aussitôt que possible,
Dans les limites du possible.
Il ne faut pas badiner avec ce genre de misère.

---

[28] Unemployment in Cameroon

Soyez rassurés,
Tous les arriérés salariaux seront payés tout de suite,
Dans les limites de nos moyens.
On ne dort pas lorsque les voisins ont
Le ventre affamé.

Faites leur confiance,
Toutes les écoles auront assez de
Fournitures bientôt,
Dans les limites de nos budgets.
Chose promise, chose due!

C'est certain,
Tous les retraités seront
Pris en charge sans plus de manières.
Personne ne végéterait devant le bâtiment
De la Caisse de la Prévoyance Sociale.
La promesse est une dette!

Il va sans dire,
Tous les sans-abri seront logés
Sans plus de cérémonie.
Nous vivons selon les préceptes
Du Contrat Social
Chose promise, chose due.
Faut toujours faire confiance
Aux élus du peuple,
Même s'ils rirent sous cape.
Ce ne sont pas les bidons vides.
On ne blague pas avec eux, hein!

Reminiscences/

Mémoires

I Had A Dream

Certainly,
Everyone delude themselves in life.
But we never know what is going to happen.
One is never sure of anything.

I had a friend
Who wanted to be a priest.
Today he is a drug-trafficker in Columbia.
He no longer believes in God.
We never know what is going to happen.
One is never sure of anything.

I had a girlfriend
Who wanted to be a reverend sister.
Today she works in a brothel in Douala.
We never know what is going to happen.
One is never sure of anything.

I had a cousin
Who wanted to be a magistrate
Today he is a *bendskin*[29] taxi driver in Bafoussam.
We never know what is going to happen.
One is never sure of anything.

I had a nephew
Who wanted to be physician
Today he is at the *Centre Jamot*[30] in Yaoundé.
We never know what is going to happen.
One is never sure of anything.

Do you know what, me,
I wanted to be when I was young?
I wanted to be diplomat.
Today I am a professor.
We never know what is going to happen.
One is never sure of anything.

---

[29] Motorcycle taxi
[30] Mental hospital in Yaoundé.

51

As I see it,
Living is dreaming.
One is never sure of anything.
You never know what is going to happen.

J'avais un rêve

Evidemment,
Tout le monde se fait des
Illusions dans la vie.
On ne sait jamais ce qui va se passer.
On n'est jamais sûr de rien.

J'avais un copain qui
Voulait être prêtre.
Aujourd'hui, il est trafiquant de drogues en Colombie.
Il ne croît plus en Dieu.
On ne sait jamais ce qui va se passer.
On n'est jamais sûr de rien.
J'avais une nana qui
Voulait prendre le voile.
Aujourd'hui, elle travaille
Dans une maison close à Douala.
On ne sait jamais ce qui va se passer.
On n'est jamais sûr de rien.

J'avais un cousin qui
Voulait être magistrat.
Aujourd'hui, il est conducteur de *bendskin* à Bafoussam.
On ne sait jamais ce qui va se passer.
On n'est jamais sûr de rien.

J'avais un neveu qui
Voulait être docteur en médecine.
Aujourd'hui il est au Centre Jamot de Yaoundé.
On ne sait jamais ce qui va se passer.
On n'est jamais sûr de rien.

Vous savez ce que je voulais être, moi,
Quand j'étais petit?
Je voulais être diplomate.
Aujourd'hui, je suis professeur.
On ne sait jamais ce qui va se passer.
On n'est jamais sûr de rien.

À mon avis,
Vivre c'est se faire des illusions.
On n'est jamais sûr de rien.
On ne sait jamais comment les choses vont tourner.

Bygone Age

I eat *foofoo-corn* with my five fingers,
Like we do at home.
Even if some people don't like it!
I don't need forks or spoons.

I drink palm wine
Out of the horn of a buffalo,
Like we do at home.
Even if some people don't like it!
I don't need glasses or cups.

I eat *njama-njama*[31] from the village
cooked in red palm oil,
Like we do at home.
Even if some people don't like it!
I don't need hotdog or hamburger.

I sleep on a bamboo bed
With dried leaves,
As we do at home.
Even if some people don't like it!
I don't need a mattress or bed-sheets.

---

[31] Huckle-berry soup

Do you realize that
Every age has its own mores?
I couldn't care less what you think!

Temps jadis

Je mange du *foofoo-corn*[32] avec mes
Cinq doigts comme chez nous.
N'en déplaise à certaines personnes!
Je n'ai besoin ni de fourchettes ni de cuillères.

Je bois du bon vin de palme
Dans la corne du buffle,
A la façon de chez nous.
N'en déplaise à certaines personnes!
Je n'ai besoin ni de verres ni de tasses.

Je mange du *njama-njama*[33] du village
Préparé avec de l'huile de palme
Comme chez nous.
N'en déplaise à certaines personnes!
Je n'ai besoin ni de hotdog
Ni de hamburger.

Je me couche sur un lit
De bambou garni des feuilles
Mortes de bananiers
A la mode de chez nous.
Je n'ai besoin ni de matelas
Ni de draps.

Vous vous en rendez compte?
Autres temps, autres moeurs.
Peu m'importe ce que
Vous en pensez!

---

[32] Balls made out of corn flour.
[33] Huckle-berry soup

54

Homage to Forebears

Oh, my ancestors!
In your time,
People ate together sitting down.
Today, things have changed,
Everyone eats in isolation,
Often standing up, ready to leave.
How the world has changed!

Oh, my ancestors!
In your time,
Grandparents lived with grandchildren,
Giving them advice on the ways of the world.
Today, things have changed,
Grandparents are quarantined in assisted-living homes
Where they spend their last days.
How the world has changed!

Oh, my ancestors!
In your time,
Youngsters heeded the advice of their parents.
Today, children do what pleases them.
How the world has changed!

Oh, my ancestors!
In your time,
A baby was considered a pearl
Today, they are unwanted creatures
To be disposed of in dumpsters.
How the world has changed!

Oh, my ancestors!
What would you say
If you had to return to this world
Full to the brim with lunatics?

Hommage aux ancêtres

Ah, mes aïeux!
A votre époque,
On mangeait ensemble assis.
Aujourd'hui, on mange seul,
 debout prêt à partir.
Que les choses ont changé!

Ah, mes aïeux!
A votre époque,
Les grand-parents vivaient ensemble
avec leurs petits-enfants.
Ils leurs donnaient des conseils sur le savoir-vivre.
Aujourd'hui, ils sont envoyés en quarantaine,
Où ils passent leurs derniers jours
Dans des maisons de retraite.
Que les choses ont changé!

Ah, mes aïeux!
A votre époque,
Les gamins tenaient compte des
Conseils de leurs parents.
Aujourd'hui, ils ne font qu'à leur tête.
Que les choses ont changé!

A votre époque,
Un bébé était considéré comme une perle.
Aujourd'hui, on jette des
Nouveau-nés dans des poubelles.
Que les choses ont changé!

Ah, mes aïeux!
Que diriez-vous
Si vous retourniez sur cette terre.
Pleine à craquer des fous?

Laughter

Do you know what laughter is all about?
The semantic ambiguity generated by
This word makes me laugh my head off!
Nevertheless, it is better to laugh than cry.
To laugh heartily,
is to laugh joyously.

Alas!

Laughter is not always pleasant.
Laugh at someone,
is to make fun of them stealthily.
Laugh up one's sleeve,
is to laugh at someone discreetly.

Laugh in someone's face
is to make fun of them.
It's tantamount to ridiculing someone.
The same holds true for
Laughing behind someone's back.

That's not all!
Laugh at the tip of one's teeth,
is to force a smile.
Laugh with one's lips
Is to fake a smile.
Laugh like a hunchback
is to be doubled up with laughter.
Laugh like a whale,
is to laugh like a drain.

With such a gamut of laughter,
How can one choose!
He that laughs last, laughs best.

Rire

Vous savez ce que c'est que rire?
L'ambiguïté de ce mot me fait
Crever de rire !
Toutefois, il vaut mieux
En rire qu'en pleurer.
Rire de bon cœur,
C'est rire joyeusement.

Hélas!

Rire, ça ne fait toujours pas plaisir:
Rire de quelqu'un
C'est se moquer de lui discrètement.
Rire sous cape,
C'est aussi rire d'une façon discrète.
Rire au nez de quelqu'un,
C'est se railler de lui.
Il en va de même pour
Rire derrière le dos de quelqu'un.

Ce n'est pas tout!
Rire du bout des dents,
C'est forcer un rire.
Rire du bout des lèvres,
C'est contrefaire un rire.
Rire comme un bossu,
C'est se tordre de rire.
Rire comme une baleine,
C'est se tenir les côtes de rire.

Avec une telle variété de rires,
Comment choisir?
Rira bien qui en rira le dernier.

Affection/Affection

A Word For My Sons
[Poem dedicated to my three sons]

Listen, my children,
Heed the advice of your father.
Be attentive in order
          to acquire a sense of discernment
              for this is good advice
                 I am giving you.
Do not ignore
My teachings
I, myself, was once a
        son to my father
        And my mother loved
           me as if I was the only child.

My sons, listen to me
And heed my words
so that you would live long.
        These are words of wisdom
          I am teaching you
             I am leading you in the right direction.

If you follow my steps
You will not falter
If you run
You will not stumble.

Hold fast onto
The education that
has been given you.

        Do not regret it
          Stay close to it
            because your survival depends on it.
Do not follow in the footsteps
Of evildoers
Do not emulate those who do evil.

61

Steer clear of their paths.
Follow in the footsteps
of the kind-hearted
For the way of the just
Is like the light of dawn.

Conseils à mes fils
[Poème dédié à mes trois fils]

Ecoutez, mes enfants,
Suivez le conseil de votre père.
Soyez attentifs pour
acquérir du discernement.
Car c'est une bonne éducation
que je vous donne.

N'abandonnez pas
mes enseignements,
Car j'ai été, moi aussi,
un fils pour mon père,
Et ma mère me chérissait
comme un enfant unique.

Mes fils, écoutez-moi
et recevez mes paroles,
ainsi vous prolongerez vos vies.
C'est la voie de la sagesse
que je vous enseigne.
Je vous guide vers de droits chemins.

Si vous y marchez,
vos pas ne serez pas gênés.
Et si vous y courez,
vous ne trébucherez pas.

Tenez-vous fermement
à l'éducation qui vous
a été donnée.

Ne le regrettez pas.
Restez-y attachés,
car vos vies en dépendent.

Ne vous engagez pas
dans la voie des méchants,
Ne suivez pas l'exemple
de ceux qui font le mal.
Eloignez-vous de leur sentier.
Le sentier des justes
est comme la lumière de l'aurore.

Advice to My Daughters
[Poem dedicated to my two daughters]

My daughters, stay close
To the precepts handed down to you by your mother.
Do not ignore the teaching of your mother.
Keep it constantly
in your hearts,
Tie it like a
Necklace around your necks!

My daughters, heed the
advice of your mother.
Do not throw away her teaching
Keep it constantly
in your hearts,
Tie it like a
Necklace around your necks!

It will be your guide
In your peregrinations
It will watch over you
in your sleep.
And will converse with you when you wake up,
For a precept is like a lamp,
And teaching like light.

Warnings and reproaches
Lead to the straight path in life
They will protect you against
Immoral men
And will put you on
your guard against
the wily words of a stranger.

Conseils à mes filles
[Ce poème est dédié à mes deux filles]

Mes filles, restez attachées
aux préceptes de votre mère.
Et ne rejettez pas
l'enseignement de votre mère.
Serrez-les constamment
dans vos coeurs,
Attachez-les comme
des colliers à vos cous!

Mes filles, restez attachées
aux conseils de votre mère.
Et ne rejetez pas
l'enseignement de votre mère.
Serrez-les constamment
dans vos coeurs,
Attachez-les comme
des colliers à vos cous!

Ils vous guideront
quand vous voyagerez
Et veilleront sur vous
durant votre sommeil.
Et s'entretiendront
avec vous à votre réveil.
Car le précepte est une lampe,
et l'enseignement une lumière.

Les avertissements
et les reproches
sont le chemin de la vie.
Ils vous préserveront
de l'homme immoral
et vous mettront en garde
contre les paroles
enjôleuses d'un inconnu.

Kola Nut

Kola nut—
Real African viagra!
Kola nut—
Pet hate of Hellenic Viagra.
Kola nut—
Viable road companion!

Kola nut—
Inexhaustible source of energy—
Energy to run;
Energy to walk;
Energy to converse;
Energy to argue;
Energy to make love;
Energy to work;
Energy to dance.
Kola nut—
Real jack of all trades!

Kola nut—
He that brings kola,
brings life.
Old African adage!

Noix de kola

Noix de kola—
Véritable aphrodisiaque africain!
Noix de kola—
Bête noire du 'viagra' hellénique.
Noix de kola—
Bon compagnon de route!

Noix de kola—
Source intarissable d'énergie—
Energie pour faire la course;
Energie pour faire la promenade;
Energie pour faire la causerie;
Energie pour faire la bagarre;
Energie pour faire l'amour;
Energie pour travailler;
Energie pour danser.
Noix de kola—
Vrai passe partout!

Noix de kola—
Qui partage la kola,
Apporte la vie,
Vieil adage africain!

Love-Sickness

Love sickness,
Has no remedy.
It's very difficult to cure.
What you've done to me,
has taught me a good lesson.

Because of you,
I will never love gain.
I wed you out of love
But you,
You married me for convenience!
What you've done to me
has taught me how to love.
Because of you,
I will never be able to love with all my heart again.
I married you for better or for worse.
But you,
You used me as stepping-stone!

Love sickness
defies all remedies.
What you've done to me,
has put me on my guard.
Because of you,
I will never have the desire to make love again.
Love malady is extremely hard to cure.

Maladie d'amour

La maladie d'amour,
N'a pas de remède.
Elle est très difficile à soigner.
Ce que tu m'as fait,
m'a donné de bonnes leçons.

A cause de toi,
je ne pourrai plus aimer.
Je t'ai épousée par amour
Mais toi,
tu m'as épousé par intérêt!
Ce que tu m'as fait,
m'a appris comment aimer.
A cause de toi,
je ne saurai plus aimer avec tout mon coeur.
Je t'ai épousé pour le meilleur et pour le pire.
Mais toi,
Tu t'es servie de moi comme marche-pied!

La maladie d'amour,
C'est très difficile à guérir.
Ce que tu as fait,
m'a mis en garde!
A cause de toi,
je ne pourrais plus avoir envie
de faire l'amour.
La maladie d'amour,
C'est fort difficile à soigner!

The Plague

What's this illness
That's eating us up day and night?
Some call it deadly honey;
Others have nicknamed it the Plague of Love.
Scientists term it AIDS.

Whatever you call it,
It has dawned on me that
This malady that's draining
our society is God's magic wand
against human misconduct.

It is written in the Sacred Book:
Watch out!
Our bodies were not made for misconduct.
The Lord is in our bodies
And we're in the Lord's body.

Do you not know that
Your bodies are part of Christ?
Do you then have to take Christ's body
And transform it into the
body of a prostitute?
I don't think so!

La peste

Quelle est cette maladie
qui nous ronge nuit et jour?
D'aucuns l'appellent le miel meurtrier.
D'autres l'ont surnommée la Peste Amoureuse.
Les scientifiques le qualifient de SIDA.

Quoi qu'il en soit,
Il m'est venu à l'esprit que
ce mal qui mine notre société,
c'est la baguette magique de Dieu
Contre l'immoralité humaine.

Il est écrit dans le Livre Sacré:
Faites attention!
Nos corps n'ont pas été faits
pour l'inconduite.
Le Seigneur est dans nos corps,
Et nous sommes dans le Corps du Seigneur.
Ignorez-vous que vos corps
sont les membres du Christ?
Faut-il donc arracher le corps
Du Christ pour en faire
celui d'une prostituée?
Je pense que non!

Love Creed

Love is like an egg,
It's very fragile.
In love, there's no room for dirty tricks,
For fear of breaking it.

Love is like a glass,
It's breakable.
In love, one should never cheat,
For fear of breaking it into a thousand pieces.
Love is like a flower
It is ephemeral.
In love partners should never
Talk at cross purposes,
For fear of crumbling it.
Love is built on mutual trust.

Love is like an apple,
You should not force it,
For fear of puncturing it.

Love is like a bird,
You should never torture it.
It could fly away for good!

LOVE... LOVE...LOVE,
WHAT A CATCH-WORD!

Credo d'amour

L'amour c'est un comme un œuf,
Il est très fragile.
En amour, il ne faut jamais
jouer de sales tours de peur de le casser.

L'amour c'est comme un verre.
Il est cassable.
En amour, il ne faut pas tricher
par peur de le briser en mille morceaux.

L'amour c'est comme une fleur.
Il est fort éphémère.
En amour, les conjoints ne doivent pas
tenir de propos contradictoires
de peur de l'effriter.
L'amour est fondé sur la confiance mutuelle.

L'amour c'est comme une pomme
Il ne faut pas le forcer.
Il risque de crever.
L'amour c'est comme un oiseau.
Il ne faut jamais le torturer,
Il risque de s'envoler pour de bon!

AMOUR... AMOUR... AMOUR,
QUEL MOT-VEDETTE!

School For Wives

A woman is not a plaything,
You don't mess with her emotions.
She can't stand inanities!
In her world,
You are friend or enemy,
No middle of the road!

It is better to live in a desert
Than share a roof with
A quarrelsome and irate woman.
An immoral wife is like a shallow well,
She is similar to an abyss full of hatred.
The shame she brings onto her husband
Is like an illness eating deep into the bone.

In Contradistinction,

A sweet wife is like
A crown on the head of her husband
Her words are like honey,
Her acts edifying.

The lips of an adulterous woman
Proffer honey-like words,
Her tongue is more soothing than oil
BUT, the evil she concocts
Is as bitter as poison.

Ecole des femmes[34]

La femme n'est pas un jouet,
Il ne faut pas badiner avec ses sentiments.
Elle ne tolère pas de sottises!
Chez la femme,
On est ami ou ennemi,
Pas de mi-chemin !

Mieux vaut habiter dans un pays désertique
Que de partager la maison
D'une femme querelleuse et irritable.
La femme immorale est comme un puits étroit,
Elle est semblable à une fosse profonde pleine de haine.
La honte quelle cause à son mari est comme
une maladie qui ronge l'os.

Par contre,
Une femme douce
est comme une couronne sur la tête de son mari.
Ses mots sont mielleux,
Ses actes sont édifiants.

Les lèvres de la femme adultère distillent
Des paroles mielleuses;
Sa langue est plus onctueuse que l'huile.
MAIS, la fin qu'elle se prépare
est aussi amère que le poison.

---

[34] Calqued on the title of Molière's comedy *L'école des femmes* (1663).